MW01166414

A Special Gift for

_____

with love,

_____

date

_____

Stories, sayings, and scriptures to Encourage and Inspire

hugs™

for

Single M❤ms

Melanie Hemry

Personalized Scriptures by
LeAnn Weiss

HOWARD BOOKS
A DIVISION OF SIMON & SCHUSTER

NEW YORK   LONDON   TORONTO   SIDNEY

OUR PURPOSE AT HOWARD BOOKS IS TO:

- *Increase faith* in the hearts of growing Christians
- *Inspire holiness* in the lives of believers
- *Instill hope* in the hearts of struggling people everywhere

Because He's Coming Again!

Published by Howard Books, a division of Simon & Schuster
1230 Avenue of the Americas, New York, NY 10020

Hugs for Single Moms © 2006 Howard Publishing Co.

Library of Congress Cataloging-in-Publication Data
Hemry, Melanie, 1949–
    Hugs for single moms : stories, sayings, and scriptures to encourage and inspire / Melanie Hemry, LeAnn Weiss.
        p. cm.
    ISBN 1-58229-484-4
    1. Single mothers—Religious life. 2. Christian women—Religious life. 3. Motherhood—Religious aspects—Christianity. I. Weiss, LeAnn. II. Title.

BV4529.18.H45 2005
242'.6431—dc22

2005054324

10 9 8 7 6 5 4 3 2

HOWARD is a registered trademark of Simon & Schuster, Inc.

Manufactured in the United States of America

For information regarding special discounts for bulk purchases, please contact Simon & Schuster Special Sales at 1-800-456-6798 or business@simonandschuster.com

Paraphrased scriptures © 2006 LeAnn Weiss, 3006 Brandywine Dr. Orlando, FL 32806; 407-898-4410

Edited by Between the Lines
Interior design by John Mark Luke Designs

Contents

Chapter 1

Being
Your Best

Even before you were born, I
specially formed you. You're My
original! I've gifted you and prepared
you in advance for the unique purposes
I created you to accomplish. You can
survive and thrive in the game of life
because I'm your power source.

Thinking precious thoughts of you,
Your Creator

—FROM PSALM 139; EPHESIANS 2:10;
PHILIPPIANS 4:13

The greatest trap for single mothers may be trying to fill someone else's shoes. The real problem is that to some extent, you're capable of doing so. For the short haul, it may even seem to work—this selfless pouring out of who you are. But the end result is often a fracturing of what you do best and a stripping of your self-confidence.

It's not that you can't fill other people's shoes. In some cases you wear them better than the one who owns them. That's not the point. The point is, you were wonderfully and gloriously made. You were created with talents and gifts as specific to you as your fingerprints. That's the well from which God designed you to draw, because it's the well of your inspiration. It's also the well of your joy, where a fountain bubbles just beneath the surface, waiting to be tapped.

Hidden within you are gifts that have never been discovered, treasures still to be mined, riches that will never run dry. When you want a new challenge, mine your well of gifts and see what you find.

The bottom line is, you are unique—one of a kind. Failing to recognize that or not living in its truth can keep you from blooming where you are. Your shoes fit you perfectly. They were made to help you run the race of life without growing weary.

Wear them well.

*B*e patient with everyone, but above all with thyself. I mean, do not be *disheartened* by your imperfections, but always *rise up* with fresh courage.

— *Francis De Saint*

For the millionth time since Dillon had died, Charlotte felt helpless to stop her sons' pain.

Back in the Game

Charlotte put the finishing touches on the cupcakes she'd made for a Boy Scout camping trip as her three sons—nine-year-old Rob and the seven-year-old twins, Jake and Jeff—walked in wordlessly and dropped onto the sofa as though they'd lost their best friend. Charlotte sighed. Actually, they had lost their best friend when their father, Dillon, died in a car wreck six months earlier. *We've all lost our best friend*, she thought with a familiar stab of pain.

"What's up, boys?"

"Mr. Klingensmith isn't going to be our coach anymore," Rob said, slamming his fist into a well-worn catcher's mitt.

"Yeah, his job is making him move to San Diego," Jeff added.

"He don't even want to go," Jake said tremulously.

Being *Your Best*

"*Doesn't* even want to go," Charlotte said automatically. She dropped into Dillon's chair and sat with the boys in speechless silence.

Other than their father, the boys' baseball coach was the single most important man in their lives. The thought of losing both of them within six months was too much to bear. For the millionth time since Dillon had died, Charlotte felt helpless to stop her sons' pain.

Dillon would have known just what to say. Charlotte was clueless, as stunned as her sons were by one more layer of loss. Before the accident—that's how Charlotte identified life events now, before the accident and after the accident— she'd been secure and confident, both as a person and as a mother. But trying to be mother and father to three boys while coping with her own grief had left her a trembling mass of insecurity.

She didn't know how to do all the great things Dillon had done. She didn't know how to turn boring chores into intergalactic adventures. She didn't know how to help Rob make a winning car for the Pinewood Derby. The one she helped him make looked something like a carrot with a tumor and hardly rolled. She couldn't even tell scary stories like Dillon had told.

"Maybe your new coach will be better than Mr. Klingensmith," she offered lamely. Three faces looked as though she were an alien with two heads. She'd done it again!

Oh boy, I've got to regroup. "Look, I'm sorry Mr. Klingensmith has to move. And, honestly, I can't imagine anyone being as good a coach as he is. I wish I could say something to make you feel better, but I don't know what it would be.

"However, you still have a camping trip tonight. That'll be fun. I've made lots of cupcakes. Why don't you go take your showers while I pack the food?" One by one, they filed out of the room.

That went well.

Later that afternoon Charlotte took pictures of them dressed in their Boy Scout uniforms before the van arrived to take them to camp. As she hugged them good-bye, Jake said, "Mom, something's wrong with my bike."

"OK, honey, I'll see what I can do."

"Bye, Mom!" All three boys climbed into the van and were gone. The house was suddenly quiet . . . too quiet.

When Dillon had been alive, Charlotte had relished snippets of time alone when the boys were gone. But now the house felt too big and too lonely.

I'd better stay busy, she thought, going outside to look at Jake's bike. She rode it around the driveway and realized immediately the chain was too loose. *I wonder how you tighten these things.* Grabbing a screwdriver, she stuck the end into the chain and tugged. Nothing.

Dillon used to adjust bicycle chains all the time. It can't be too tough, she thought as she turned the bicycle upside down. Turning the pedal, she looked for a way to tighten the chain. Nothing.

For forty-five minutes she poked, prodded, tugged, and pulled. She had grease in her hair and on her hands, her face, and her sweatshirt. Choking back a sob, she shut the garage door and went into the house.

In the bathroom Charlotte washed the grease off of her hands and face and watched it run like mascara down the sink. *Just like my best efforts.*

After drying her hands and face, she stepped into her favorite sanctuary—Dillon's closet. She'd given a lot of his clothes to his brother, but she'd kept his favorite plaid flannel shirt. Dillon had worn it on Saturdays to rake leaves, play ball with the boys, or wash the car.

Removing her grease-stained sweatshirt, Charlotte put on the worn flannel shirt. The sleeves hung down over her fingertips, and the hem fell below her knees. Gathering the folds and holding them to her face, she breathed in Dillon's scent. This ritual had been her secret comfort for six months. She would never get rid of his Saturday shirt.

Back in the Game

She remembered all the delicious Saturdays they'd spent together when they were dating. They'd met in college, where Dillon pitched for the men's baseball team and Charlotte pitched for the women's softball team. It was their love of the sport that drew them together initially. Instead of romantic dinners and movies, their courtship had consisted of hot dogs and sodas at an endless lineup of ball games. When they weren't attending a ball game, they were talking about one. On many fall Saturdays they stood among swirling leaves and practiced their pitches.

A pair of Dillon's shoes caught Charlotte's eye. For some reason she stepped into them. When she caught her reflection in the mirror on the closet door, she laughed out loud. She looked like the clown that had shaped balloon animals at the school fair.

Stepping closer to the mirror, Charlotte felt as she had at five years old, trying to walk in her father's shoes. They'd been so massive she couldn't even lift them. Each time she'd tried to take a step, her foot had slipped out of the shoe.

"Those shoes don't fit."

Charlotte stood perfectly still. Where had those words come from? Was Dillon or God trying to tell her something? She stood in the quiet house, listening.

That was it; there was nothing more.

Being *Your Best*

Those shoes don't fit.

What was that supposed to mean?

Of course! Dillon's shoes didn't fit. For six long months she'd been trying to walk in Dillon's shoes. She'd tried to fill as many of the voids created by his loss as possible, and she'd failed miserably—because his shoes didn't fit.

No matter how desperately she wanted to stop her sons' pain at losing their father, she couldn't do it. There was only one Dillon.

But there was also only one Charlotte.

"I've got to stop trying to walk in Dillon's shoes," she said aloud. "I've got to wear my own shoes and figure out what works for me."

Like bicycle chains—fixing them didn't work for her, and she had to stop beating herself up over it. That's why she'd lost her confidence. Charlotte slipped her feet out of Dillon's shoes and put them in a stack of things going to the church rummage sale.

Sitting on the floor of the closet, Charlotte put on her own sneakers and tied the laces in her signature bow. Then, pulling her cell phone out of her pocket, she called Dillon's brother.

"I hate to bother you," she said, "but we have a problem.

Back in the Game

Jake's bicycle chain is loose, and I can't figure out how to fix it."

Charlotte was surprised at how genuinely glad Dillon's brother sounded when she asked for his help. He promised to come over later that day.

People want to help, she realized. All she had to do was ask.

Marking that chore off of her mental to-do list, Charlotte sat down and made a new list. Instead of trying to be Dillon, she made a list of her own strengths and gifts. She would draw from the things she *could* do.

A few minutes later she sat back with a satisfied smile. Then she made one last call.

The following week Charlotte sat on the bleachers and watched the boys' baseball practice. There were no high-fives or horsing around among the team members. Rob dragged his bat in the dirt as he walked—shoulders slumped—to the field. Jake and Jeff both watched Mr. Klingensmith as though he were a phantom who might disappear at any moment. Even Mr. Klingensmith's friendly jibes did nothing to lift the mood. It seemed none of their hearts were in the game. Finally Mr. Klingensmith called everyone to the sidelines.

"Listen up," he said. "You all know this is my last practice before I move. So I want to introduce you to your new coach."

A tense pause of expectancy hung in the air. Twelve pairs of eyes scanned the area as if searching for their first glimpse of the mystery man who would try to take Mr. Klingensmith's place.

Charlotte realized she was holding her breath as she studied her boys' reactions. She slowly released her breath and stood, then ran down the steps and onto the field.

She could see her sons looking past her, trying to see around her to their new coach. And then she savored the sweet moment when shocked understanding finally registered on their faces. "Mom?" All three boys' jaws dropped.

"But she's a girl!" the catcher, Brandon, objected.

"Yeah!" several other voices chimed in.

"My mom was the best pitcher in the minor leagues," Rob said defensively. "My dad said so, and my dad don't lie."

"Doesn't lie," Charlotte said gently, inwardly grateful for Rob's support. She smiled at him and was pleased to see—was that a hint of pride in his eyes? "OK, team, let's get started. We have a lot of work to do."

This was work Charlotte felt confident she could handle. It felt good to be back in the game.

"Batter up!"

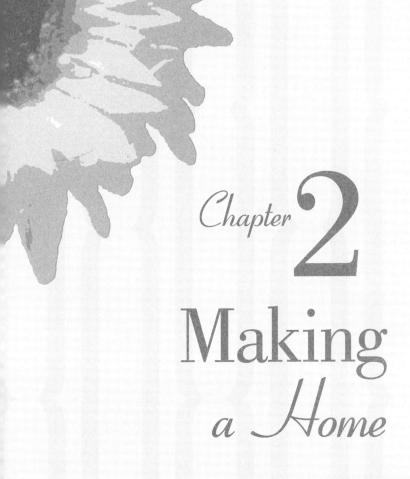

Chapter **2**

Making
a Home

In Me you live and breathe and experience life. Let My unfailing love be your comfort. Just as you comfort your child, I comfort you. I comfort you in every situation so you can reach out and help others by sharing the comfort I've given you. Never forget that I'm your way, your truth, and your life, always.

Forever faithful,
Your Ever-Present God

—FROM ACTS 17:28; PSALM 119:76; ISAIAH 66:13;
2 CORINTHIANS 1:3–4; JOHN 14:6

19

Nesting is an essential part of mothering. It's instinctive to try to create a snug place where we can hover over our little ones until they're strong enough to fly away. We want a home tough enough to withstand the rigors of life but soft enough to cushion a child's hard landing. And in that space we want things that comfort. Like the scent of spaghetti simmering on the stove, a pie cooling on the table, or a freshly brewed pot of coffee. Familiarity brings comfort as well: a familiar picture, a familiar plate, or a familiar vase of flowers. Just as we enjoy the comfort of a soft robe, an old pair of slippers, or a chair that has shaped itself to fit us, a familiar house can feel like an old friend. That's why there's nothing like going home.

It's that nesting instinct that makes it hard to transplant children and put down new roots. Families are a lot like plants: they bloom best when their roots go deep. Sometimes even transplanting to better soil—new places, new habits, new traditions— can shock the vine.

Yet the traditions your child holds so dearly are not really about places or things. The comfort comes from the fact that you cared enough to carry on those traditions year after year. So during seasons of change, when nothing seems familiar or fun, remember this: You are what makes "home" home. You are the roots. You are the familiar splash of love that spells comfort in your child's life.

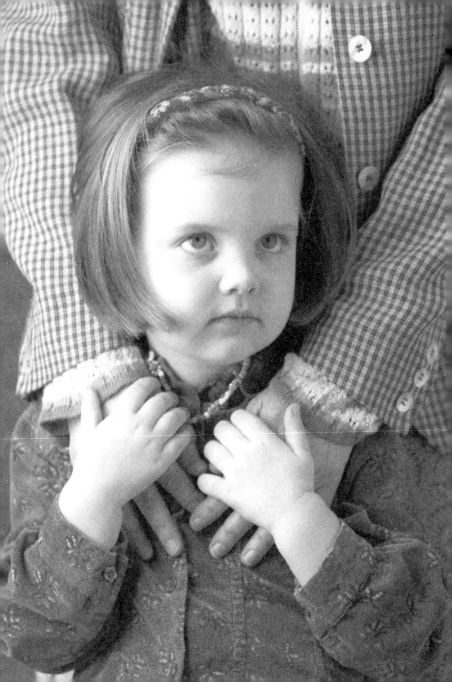

Be grateful for the home
you have, *knowing* that at
this moment, all you have
is *all* you need.

–*Sarah Ban Breathnach*

The time had come for Grace to practice what she'd preached. She only hoped she'd been right all these years.

Home for the Holidays

The Christmas lights that dotted downtown didn't twinkle. They seemed to blink periodically, as if unsure about the whole jolly thing. An angel hovered above Main Street, but the lights on one wing had gone out. *I know just how that angel must feel,* Grace thought, glancing at her twelve-year-old daughter, Katelyn, who stared miserably out the car window.

"Have you started your Christmas wish list yet?" Grace asked with forced cheerfulness.

Katelyn sighed deeply. "No. It doesn't seem like Christmas here. Back home we'd be watching the lights reflect off the lake at Ski Island. We'd go see the tree in Leadership Square. We'd be with the rest of the family at Grandma's house. Aunt Karen would roast the turkey. Aunt Barb would bring her pear pie. Connie would make pumpkin bread that melts in your mouth. *That's* Christmas." The longing on her face was so poignant, Grace had to look away.

Yeah, but I got a big promotion to move here, Grace wanted to say. We're finally out of that dingy little apartment and living in our own home. I even have money in a 401(k). But she didn't say any of those things, because right now she'd trade everything in her retirement plan to be back home, surrounded by the people she loved.

"Sounds to me like you're hungry," Grace said with a smile. "Are you in the mood for pizza?"

"Sure," Katelyn replied, leaning her head against the seat and closing her eyes.

There was no point in telling Katelyn that Christmas here would be merry, because Thanksgiving had been an unmitigated disaster. Living too far away to go home for the holidays, Grace had prepared a turkey and even attempted a pear pie. But without family and friends, the food lost its flavor and the day seemed endless. It was certainly not the kind of day that triggered fond memories and thankful attitudes.

"Here are some lights," Grace said hopefully as they passed Rudolph perched atop a roof with his red nose glowing like a nuclear reactor.

"Hmm . . . ," Katelyn said, never opening her eyes.

Home for the Holidays

OK, so maybe this outing hadn't been an effective time of bonding. Katelyn wasn't clinically depressed, but she'd sure lost her spark since moving here. As a social worker Grace was well aware that depression and suicide soared during the holidays. For many people everything about the season is a stark reminder that their lives are not filled with people they love, and Christmas is not merry. For the first time Grace and Katelyn were getting a little taste of that reality.

Katelyn had always been the kind of kid who would squeal over a blinking traffic light during the holidays. Now Grace had watched her sink into isolation, and the Christmas season only seemed to make things worse, not better.

Grace had frequently counseled others that one effective way to combat the blues was to help someone less fortunate. It usually helped people put their own problems in perspective. The time had come for Grace to practice some of what she had preached to others. She only hoped she'd been right all these years—for Katelyn's sake, and for her own.

"I stopped by the community center this afternoon," Grace said tentatively, unsure how Katelyn would respond. She ignored the fact that her daughter never opened her eyes and didn't appear to be listening. "They gave me the name of a little girl who won't be getting anything for Christmas."

Katelyn didn't respond.

"Her name's Alicia."

Silence.

"Poor little girl," Grace persevered. "Her house burned down, and her family lost everything."

"Everything?" Katelyn asked, raising her head and opening her eyes. "A fire. Wow. What a bummer."

"What would you think about taking part of our Christmas money and buying something for her?" Grace asked.

Katelyn shrugged. "That'd be OK, I guess. As long as she doesn't think we're some kind of do-gooders who believe we're better . . . you know?"

"Well, maybe we could do it anonymously."

"I like that idea," Katelyn said thoughtfully. "We'd have to be sneaky."

"Alicia's nine, so you'll know better than I would what she'd like," Grace explained. "Let's figure out how much we can spend, and I'll trust you to do the shopping."

"They lost everything?"

"That's what I was told."

Katelyn leaned her head against the window and closed her eyes. "A fire would be worse than moving."

It was Christmas Eve, and Grace had been pleasantly surprised by the excitement with which Katelyn embraced their Christmas project. Grace unpacked boxes of Christmas ornaments from the attic while Katelyn filled the kitchen table with wrapping paper, ribbon, and the gifts she'd purchased for Alicia.

"I can't wait to show you what I bought!" Katelyn actually sounded excited.

"Those bags can't all be for Alicia," Grace said. "I didn't give you that much money!"

"I only bought things on sale, and I did really good," Katelyn said, beaming.

"Don't keep me in suspense! Let's see!"

"I thought about what you would still have if everything burned up," Katelyn explained. "You would still have your thoughts and feelings."

"I guess that's right."

"So I bought Alicia a diary that locks, so she can write down her thoughts and feelings and keep them forever."

"What a great idea."

"That's not all," Katelyn said, her brown eyes sparkling. "I thought if I lost everything, I wouldn't feel very special. So I bought her this cool pink sweater that says Princess."

"It's so cute!"

"Wait, I've got something else. I figured she needed a new book bag, and look what I found." Katelyn pulled from a bag a pink and black backpack. "And this was on the clearance table," she said, brandishing a new Barbie.

"Katelyn, I'm amazed at all you bought and how you made the money stretch!"

Katelyn looked pleased, but not as pleased as Grace felt as they wrapped the gifts in bright Christmas paper. She could tell her daughter was happy because of the relaxed, fun way she talked about Alicia, the gifts, and her shopping experience.

Later, after dark, Grace parked the car down the street from the little rental house where Alicia's family was staying. Mother and daughter crept across the yard and placed the gifts on the front porch.

"Ready?" Katelyn whispered with a nervous grin. When Grace nodded, Katelyn pressed the doorbell, and they sprinted back down the street. From a safe distance they saw light from the living room spill onto the porch when someone opened the front door.

Back in the car, they laughed and tried to catch their breath. "You ran into a shrub!" Katelyn said, pulling leaves out of her mother's hair.

"I know! I turned to look back and ran right into a big old bush." They were still laughing when they got home.

"Come on, kiddo," Grace tousled Katelyn's hair affectionately. "It's time to decorate our own Christmas tree." Grace and Katelyn exclaimed over every familiar old ornament. "My mom gave this to me for my sixteenth birthday," Grace said as she held up a red, tear-shaped ornament that said Sweet Sixteen.

"And here's the Rudolph ornament I made out of a clothespin in first grade," Katelyn said, laughing as she hung Rudolph in a place of honor.

"Oh look, this is a plaster cast of your hand in preschool." Grace held the ornament carefully.

Katelyn set the large wooden soldier on top of the television where he'd stood sentinel over every Christmas for years.

"I know we always exchange gifts on Christmas morning," Grace said. "But if you don't object, I'd like to switch to Christmas Eve and open them tonight."

"How come?" Katelyn asked guardedly.

"There's going to be a free Christmas meal served at the community center tomorrow morning, and they need volunteers. I thought we might help."

"I don't know," Katelyn said, scrunching her face into a grimace. "What would I have to do?"

"I'm not sure. Probably help set up tables and serve food."

"I guess," she said with a less than enthusiastic shrug.

"Hey," she sniffed the air suddenly. "Do I smell spaghetti?"

"Yes," Grace admitted with a sigh. "I decided not to try to compete with Aunt Karen's turkey. So I made spaghetti with meatballs, garlic toast, a salad, and Aunt Barb's pear pie."

"No turkey?" Katelyn asked, an incredulous look on her face. "No ham or sweet potatoes?"

Suddenly Grace was uneasy. All the goodwill and holiday spirit she'd sensed in Katelyn seemed poised to crash in on her with this last straw. She braced herself for Katelyn's disappointment.

"I *hate* eating turkey for weeks after the holiday," Katelyn said with an animated voice. "I *love* having spaghetti for Christmas!"

Christmas morning passed in a blur of activity as they set up tables and chairs, unloaded plates from a walk-in pantry, stirred huge pots of food—and sliced one pear pie. It had been Katelyn's idea to give it away, just one more indication to Grace of how far her daughter's attitude had come.

Long lines had formed outside the building by the time the doors were opened. Grace served mashed potatoes and gravy while Katelyn placed a scoop of dressing on each plate. Grace was proud of the compassionate and friendly way

Katelyn truly looked at, smiled at, and greeted each person she served.

"Merry Chris—" The words froze on Katelyn's lips. Curious, Grace looked up to see a little girl with blond hair and blue eyes. She wore a pink sweater that said Princess, had slung over her shoulder a pink and black backpack, and held a Barbie under one arm.

Katelyn glanced at her mother with a stunned look on her face. Then turning back to the little girl, she said, "Hi! I mean, Merry Christmas!"

"Santa found my house," the little girl said shyly. "I didn't think he would. See what I got?" She held up her Barbie and turned to model her sweater and backpack.

"Wow, that's great," Katelyn said with a smile.

That smile didn't go away the entire afternoon that Grace and Katelyn served, talked, put away food, and cleaned up the community center. Then, in satisfied silence, they drove back to the house. The lights on their little tree were blinking merrily in the window. Once inside, Katelyn threw herself onto the sofa with an exhausted moan. "Oh . . . it feels so good to be home."

Grace looked around the new house with surprise.

Home? Yes, home. It was *good to be home.*

Chapter 3

Juggling Life

In this world you'll face many challenges. Just remember, you're not alone. I am for you. Nothing can ever separate you from My incomparable love. I'll never leave you or forsake you.

Loving you always,
Your Awesome God

—FROM JOHN 16:33; ROMANS 8:31, 38–39; DEUTERONOMY 31:6

As a single mom you may be one of the greatest tightrope walkers who ever lived. Even you don't know how you manage to balance and juggle so many things. Nor do you know how you can be so many things to so many people. You take multitasking to a whole new level. Yet somehow you make it look easy, for there is a grace in your life.

It's OK to feel like taking a bow at the next Academy Awards ceremony. We'd all like to see the most accomplished actress try to pull off your role. You laugh when you feel like crying. You're strong though you feel weak. You allow others to lean on you when you'd like—just for a little while— to do some leaning yourself.

inspirational message

It would be fun, though, to sometimes change circumstances: to never again have to worry about bouncing a check or making the mortgage payment. It would be nice to have someone else clean your refrigerator, buy your groceries, and mop your floors.

But it's doubtful you'd ever consider changing roles: not with Donald Trump or Bill Gates, in spite of their mansions and millions. Because they have never been, nor will they ever become, a mother. For all its difficulties and challenges, yours is the role you were created to fill. You are the leading lady on the stage of your child's life, and that's worth everything. Go ahead . . . take a bow.

The woman who creates and sustains a *home* and under whose hands children grow up to be *strong* and *pure* men and women, is a *creator* second only to God.

—Helen Hunt Jackson

Of all the times to take an emotional nosedive! What am I going to do about my presentation?

Love Languages

Stephanie booted up her laptop and opened her briefcase stuffed with memos, bids, and proposals. She stifled a yawn as freezing rain pelted the window. She wanted nothing more than to put on flannel pajamas, make a cup of hot chocolate, wrap up in an old quilt, and curl up on the sofa in front of a roaring fire.

"Not gonna happen," she muttered, taking a sip of the coffee she'd brewed to help her stay awake. It had been a long day. More accurately, it had been a long, hard year of trying to land a new account for her company. For months she'd worked extra hours, even going back to the office on weekends to tie up loose ends.

The presentation she would make tomorrow would be the *coup de grâce*. Within twenty-four hours everyone would know whether her efforts had paid off. As if that weren't enough pressure, her boss had called her into his office today and shut the door.

"Stephanie," he'd said, "the company's future is in your hands. Closing this deal will make the difference between growth and expansion or downsizing. We're counting on you."

Hey, but no pressure! she thought. *I knew we hadn't made quota, but I had no idea the company might have to downsize. I can't afford to lose this job!*

The crunch of tires on ice alerted her that her parents had arrived to drop off her five-year-old son, Wiley. *They've kept him at their house a lot during my late hours these past months,* she thought with a spasm of remorse. *This project's almost complete,* she reminded herself. *I'll let him watch* Scooby-Doo *tonight while I work.*

A blast of frigid air nearly took Stephanie's breath away when she opened the door for Wiley. "Hey, Sport!" she said, pushing back the hood of his jacket. His eyes were puffy and swollen from crying. Still dripping with rain, he launched himself into her arms.

"Did you have a rough day at kindergarten?" she asked, easing him out of his coat and then holding him close. He nodded, burying his face in her shoulder.

"Wiley, whatever happened at school today, I'll help you. That's why children have mommies, to help them. Do you remember when I told you that?"

"Yeah."

"OK. Now what happened?"

Wiley stood back to explain. "Ya know how I'm the Indian chief?"

"In the school play tomorrow? Yes, I know."

"Well, I can't say my words." His blue eyes brimmed with tears again.

"Aren't you supposed to say, 'Welcome Pilgrims! I bring you great bounty'?"

"Yeah, 'cept I can't say *pilgwims*, and all the kids laughed at me," he confessed, lips trembling. "And my Indian chief clothes was too big, and I accidentally stepped on it and fell down. Then I dropped the corn and punkins, and they rolled everywhere, and even Mrs. White laughed. She turned around, but I saw."

Wiley buried his face in Stephanie's neck and sobbed in mortification. "And now my Indian clothes is torn, and I don't have nothin' to wear."

Stephanie closed her eyes and felt like sobbing with him. *Oh Lord, don't let him have a meltdown! I can't handle it today!* He sobbed until his cries turned to hiccups and sniffles.

"I'll bet I know what happened," Stephanie said.

Big blue eyes moist with tears looked up at her. "What?"

"I'll bet you forgot to wear your Batman costume when you practiced your lines last night."

"My costume?" he asked, blinking at the mention of his favorite outfit.

"Well, sure. You can't wear it in the play, but if you wear it when you practice, you can be Batman in disguise tomorrow."

"OK," he said, giving her a teary smile and dashing to his room to put on his pointed black mask and cape. Stephanie focused on the blank computer document and wrote the opening line of her presentation.

"I'm Batman!" Wiley announced as he raced into the room, flexing his muscles.

"OK, Batman, it's time to practice your lines. Did you eat all your dinner tonight?"

"Yeah."

"Then I'll fix you some warm milk and graham crackers for a snack while you practice your lines in your room." If only Wiley's crackers and assignment would keep him occupied for a while, she could make some real progress.

Quiet fell over the apartment, and Stephanie returned to work on her presentation. A short time later, as she absentmindedly munched on a leftover cracker, her concentration was broken by the sound of Wiley weeping. *Oh no . . . not now!* Stephanie leaned her head into her hands and moaned. She walked into Wiley's room and sat next to him on his bed. "Hey, Batman, what's wrong?"

Wiley set his face in an exasperated pout. "I still can't say *pilgwim*."

"So what? You're so cute that everyone will love the way you say it."

"Nuh-uh . . . they'll laugh. I know they will."

"I don't understand why you can't say the *R* in *pilgrim* when you can say the *R* in other words."

"It's cause I got a mental lock," Wiley explained.

Stephanie worked very hard not to smile. "It's called a mental block. OK, let me help you."

Thirty minutes later a frustrated Stephanie glanced at the clock and stifled a groan. Of all the times to take an emotional nosedive! *What am I going to do about my presentation?* No matter how many ways she tried to help him, Wiley couldn't wrap his tongue around the *R* in *pilgrim*.

"Pretend you're Tony the Tiger and say, 'Great!'"

"Gweat!" Wiley exclaimed.

"G-rrr-eat!"

"Gweat!"

"OK, let me think of an *R* word you can say," Stephanie mused. "I know! Can you say *grin*?"

"Grin!" Wiley shouted.

"That's great!"

"Grin!" he repeated, beaming.

"Now say *grim*."

"Gwim."

Stephanie let out a long sigh, trying not to get a mental block of her own. "OK," she said. "Say *pill*."

"Pill."

"Now look in my eyes and say *grin*," Stephanie said with a huge smile.

"Grin," Wiley said, grinning back.

"Now say *pil-grin*," Stephanie urged.

"Pil-grin," Wiley repeated. "What does it mean?"

"It means that sometimes you're a little pill, but most of the time you make me grin." She rubbed his head affectionately.

"Is that the right way to say it?"

"No one will laugh. Now, you need a costume." Stephanie went to her closet and pulled out an old robe the color of doe eyes. Cutting it down the seam, she made a soft brown tunic and pants just Wiley's size.

Wiley's lip trembled when she tucked him into bed. "Mom, what if . . ."

"Son, look at my eyes."

"Pil-grin!" he said, a grin spreading across his face.

"That's right, chief. And don't forget I'll be there for your play."

"You won't be late?"

"And miss my son becoming a star? I don't think so!"

Stephanie could hardly keep her eyes open when she went back to her laptop and resumed working on her presentation. Finally, in the wee hours of the morning, she crawled into bed with a groan of exhaustion.

Stephanie's cell phone rang persistently—accusingly—as she hurried into the school auditorium. She glanced at the caller ID and recognized her boss's cell-phone number. She hesitated just a moment, took a deep breath, and turned off the ringer. White knuckles tightened into a fist around the cell phone. She knew in her heart that her boss was calling to yell at her for blowing the big deal—and her chances for continued employment. With a mixture of resoluteness and great sadness, Stephanie decided her boss would just have to wait until after Wiley's program to fire her. *That was the best job I've ever had*, she thought wistfully.

Her afternoon presentation had gone well; she was sure of that. So well that the president of the other company had wanted to discuss her ideas over dinner. Stephanie's boss had given her a look that clearly communicated, "Let's go to dinner and close this deal!"

"We'd love to, wouldn't we, Stephanie?" he'd said before she could answer.

For the space of a heartbeat, Stephanie had felt like a deer caught in headlights. What should she do? If she went to dinner, she'd miss the play and let Wiley down. If she attended Wiley's play, she'd be letting down her boss—and the company. She'd probably lose the deal . . . and her job.

"I'd like nothing more," she'd said warmly. "But I'm afraid I'll have to take a rain check. I have a date with the most important man in my life. My five-year-old son is the Indian chief who welcomes the pilgrims in his school play tonight, and I don't want to miss his debut. You two go on to dinner without me. After all, Bill is the brains behind this operation."

She'd felt her boss's eyes drilling holes in her back as she left.

Now she took a deep breath and forced herself to put it all aside to focus on Wiley.

Stephanie made her way down the aisle toward the front of the packed auditorium. Just moments later Wiley stepped onto the stage in his new costume. He wore a feather head-dress and carried a basket filled with ears of corn, acorn squash, and pumpkins. Stephanie saw him searching the audience for her, and she stepped forward. The movement caught his eye, and he looked relieved. He grinned at her. She held her breath, anxious for him to do well.

"Welcome, pil-grin! I bring you great bounty." With a flourish, he presented the food to the pilgrims.

Stephanie's relief and excitement at Wiley's triumph was evident on her face. She hoped her wide smile would let the little boy know just how proud she was. Pictures! She needed to take pictures. She dug her cell phone from her purse and took several snapshots. As the program concluded and every-one took a final bow, Stephanie moved to the front to get a closeup of her little chief. Her breath caught as she noticed a text message from her boss. It was too late to keep from reading it.

"We closed the deal. Great work."

Before the message could totally sink in, she was at the stage. Wiley launched himself into her arms like a torpedo.

"I did it, Mom," he exclaimed jubilantly. "I did it!"

Stephanie hugged him tight and whirled around in a circle. "You sure did, Batman! And I did too!"

Chapter 4

Letting
Go

You're blessed when you acclaim Me and walk in the light of My presence. I'll instruct you and teach you in the way you should go. Trust Me to counsel you and watch over your family. Remember, the children of the righteous are never forsaken.

Holding you safe in My arms,
Your Mighty Refuge

—FROM PSALMS 89:15; 32:8; 37:25

If you think about it, the whole process of childbirth and child rearing is about separation. The first and scariest separation for the child comes when he or she is unceremoniously thrust out of the protective cocoon of the mother's womb. That first letting go sets the tempo of a waltz that mother and child will dance for years to come. Step one: nine months of nurturing right under mother's heart. Step two: thrust from the quiet warmth to bright lights and loud noises. Step three: tenderly rocked at mother's breast. Step four: urged to try another step after falling.

It's the rhythm of mothers and children throughout the ages: We hold children tight and then let them go in miniscule

inspirational message

increments—because none of us could otherwise bear it. We teach children to be our helpers
at home and then thrust them into a scary world.
We teach them to love their family so they can leave
and build one of their own.

Every step of parenting—from nursing to nursing
home—is about letting go. As a mother your heart
yearns to hold, yet you possess the wisdom to help
your young ones launch out into new waters. In the
process you must be doctor, nurse, and guidance counselor. You are the balm to mend
a broken heart. You hold your children
close even while urging them on. You
give your children roots even as you
inspire their dreams. You are a
paradox. You are a mentor.

You are Mom.

In the final analysis it is not what you do for your *children* but what you have taught them to do for *themselves* that will make them successful human beings.

—*Ann Landers*

Victoria felt as though she were losing something of great importance—her role as mother and protector.

Dr. Mom

The mantel clock struck the hour and chimed as Victoria fingered the veil onto which she'd just finished hand-stitching pearls. *One o'clock. And one month to go.* She held the shimmering folds and blinked back tears. Where had the time gone? Like the minutes ticking away on the mantel clock, the years had passed too quickly. It seemed as though God had set her world on the spin cycle, and the joyful days of raising Lauren were over too soon.

Hanging the veil in a protective bag next to Lauren's wedding dress, Victoria went outside and dropped to her knees in the rich, dark soil. Gardening always had been both her favorite hobby and her best therapy. There was something about putting her hands into the earth that made her feel well grounded.

Letting *Go*

Red geraniums, yellow snapdragons, pink roses, and blue creeping heather all lifted their faces to the sun. *I know how to bandage bruised knees,* she thought as she snipped dead heads off the roses. *I know how to teach a kid to spell and ride a bike. I know how to comfort a broken heart. I know how to dress her for prom and pack her for college. I just don't know how to let go.*

There, she'd admitted it.

"I thought I'd find you out here," Lauren's voice interrupted Victoria's reverie.

"You're home earlier than I expected," Victoria said, motioning her daughter into a nearby lawn chair.

Lauren plopped down and let out a long sigh. "Mom, I don't know what my problem is. After graduating from medical school, planning a wedding should be a piece of cake—even an outdoor wedding," she added, looking up at the cloudless sky. "Drake and I spent the morning visiting floral shops, which was discouraging. Then I realized it was because none of their flowers looked as good as yours. If you don't mind, I'd like to raid yours for the wedding."

Victoria let her gaze wander over the half acre of landscaped flower beds. "I can't think of a more fitting use for them. Cross that off your list. What else is bothering you?"

Dr. Mom

"Drake's mother called this morning and said she had a wedding present for me," Lauren said with a noticeable lack of enthusiasm.

"Let's see," Victoria said, holding up four fingers. "Doesn't that make four?"

"My point exactly."

Victoria chuckled. "Let her have fun, honey. They're certainly wealthy enough to afford it, and she doesn't have a daughter. You're filling that void."

"I suppose."

"So what was the gift?"

"You'll never believe it," Lauren said, kneeling beside her mother and ripping off dead flowers. "She hired a string quartet for the wedding. She said it would give the wedding more charm."

Victoria grimaced. "That's not exactly what you had in mind, is it?"

"Not in the least," Lauren grumbled. "I feel like she has practically taken over the wedding."

Victoria frowned. "What are you going to do?"

"I'm not going to let her run my life, no matter how good her intentions," Lauren said. "But I'm going to pick my battles. I don't think a battle over a string quartet is worth the stress of going to war just before the wedding."

"I agree," Victoria said. "Besides, I think a string quartet will be charming." Lauren's cell phone rang, and she waved a quick good-bye before leaving for her shift at the hospital.

I'm going to miss our talks, Victoria thought, feeling the emptiness of the house already. To save money while attending medical school, Lauren had moved back home. Not that she spent much time there, with her on-call schedule. But Victoria enjoyed making her breakfast after Lauren's long night shifts. *It isn't just Lauren's life that's changing. Mine is shifting as well.* She knew it was a natural thing, a good thing, and for the most part, she was overjoyed. But a big part of her still felt as though she were losing something of great importance—not just Lauren, but her role as mother and protector. She would get used to her new role. She was determined to let go—for Lauren's sake.

The next two and a half weeks were a blur of ordinary life and the detailed preparations for that most extraordinary day. One night, just more than a week before the wedding, Lauren came home from the hospital late and more agitated than usual, even considering the nearness of the big event. Eager for every last opportunity to help, Victoria made a snack for the two of them while Lauren changed out of her scrubs.

Dr. Mom

"You won't believe what she's done now!" Lauren's voice was an octave higher than usual when she plopped onto the sofa.

Victoria knew immediately that Drake's mother, Norma, must have crossed some boundary line for Lauren to be this upset. "What now?" she asked.

"She said we have to make the center aisle five feet wider."

"And that would be because—"

"Because she's hired a white carriage pulled by two white horses, and she wants me to ride in it to the altar!" Fury tipped Lauren's words. "I might as well ride in a pumpkin!"

Victoria tried to stop the laughter that bubbled up inside, but it was too late.

"You're laughing?" Lauren was indignant.

"I'm sorry," Victoria said, still gasping with laughter. "But your grandfather is supposed to walk you down the aisle. I suddenly pictured him astride a white horse."

Lauren chuckled at the mental image, and then burst out laughing.

When they both caught their breath, Lauren turned serious again. "Mom, what am I going to do? Why is Norma acting this way?"

Letting *Go*

"I'm not sure," Victoria answered. "You've known her for years. Has she ever been controlling?"

"No. That's why I can't figure out what's going on."

"I think I might know," Victoria said with a sigh, realizing the truth was hitting awfully close to home. "She may simply be having trouble letting go. She probably feels Drake doesn't need her anymore, so she's trying to create a need and fill it."

"You think?"

"I do."

"You're a great diagnostician. What's the treatment, Dr. Mom?"

"First, think of things you really need Norma to do, and keep her busy. Next, suggest that Drake take her to lunch and spend some extra time with her. And about the carriage; I think it might be a lovely substitute for the limousine that's supposed to take you to the wedding. Think about it, and if you like the idea, you could let the carriage drop you off where Grandpa will meet you. If you really don't want the carriage, simply be gracious, thank her, and explain that you've already made other arrangements."

"Do you make house calls?"

"Just for special people," Victoria said with a smile.

"Thanks, Mom. We may still be able to salvage our wedding plans—and my relationship with my future mother-in-law." They sat in comfortable silence for a while before Lauren spoke again.

"I think you're right about Norma," she said thoughtfully. "She probably feels insecure because her role in Drake's life is changing. I don't know why I didn't figure it out for myself, because I think that's the same reason I've been fractious and fearful. Drake hasn't quite been himself either. With our marriage, the role of every important person in our lives is shifting."

Victoria nodded, letting silence wrap them both like a blanket.

"You'll laugh when I tell you what keeps coming to my mind," Lauren said, a smile tugging at her lips.

"What?"

"My first piano recital," she said, laughing.

Victoria shook her head and laughed at the memory. "It was horrible! Of course, you did get better with time, but I can't tell you how relieved I was when you excelled in science. You didn't have much of a future in music!"

They both laughed for several minutes before Lauren turned misty eyes to her mother. "There's something I need to tell you," she said. "You know I'm normally a courageous person. I wasn't afraid of going to medical school, but leaving my home and you for good has unnerved me. Today I feel as scared as I did at my first piano recital."

"Oh, honey—"

"Let me finish. I thought about it all morning and finally realized what's been scaring me. It's that you won't be beside me. You've stood by me during every major event in my life. You're the reason I made it through that piano recital. You helped me through geometry. You convinced me I'd survive when I got dumped on prom night.

"On the most important day of my life, I need you beside me. In fact, I don't think I can walk down the aisle otherwise. I've already called Grandpa and told him how I feel. He understood. So Mom . . . would you give me away?"

Images flashed through Victoria's mind: Lauren's first tooth, her first step, running alongside her bicycle until she was able to ride solo, her first broken heart, and now this—the most momentous first step in her life.

Lauren was no longer an infant, a toddler, or a teen. She was a beautiful woman, ready to launch out into the rest of her life. Victoria had loved every moment of those bygone years, but she didn't want to miss a second of Lauren's life as a woman, a wife—a friend.

Dr. Mom

"All you've got to do is walk me down the aisle." Lauren was talking fast, as she always did when she was nervous or scared. "You know, just get me down there. Then the minister will say, 'Who gives this woman in marriage?' And you'll say—"

"I do!" Victoria said emphatically.

I really, really do!

Chapter **5**

Opening
Your Heart

My compassions for you never fail; they are fresh every morning. Remember, I purposely created this day. Joyfully celebrate today! Watch Me transform your tears and disappointments into songs of joy. You can be sure that My plans for you include hope and a future. After you suffer, I will restore you and make you strong, firm, and steadfast.

Restoring your soul,
Your God of Grace

—FROM LAMENTATIONS 3:22–23; PSALMS 118:24; 126:5; JEREMIAH 29:11; 1 PETER 5:10

It's easy, when you've been hurt, to put up walls to guard your emotions and protect you from pain. The problem is that sometimes it backfires. While walls might keep certain types of pain at bay, they can also block opportunities for joy. They can keep you from seeing the great gift of each new day and the blessing of rich, new relationships.

Sure, it's tough when disappointment hardens your heart and pain adds another layer of doubt and distrust. There's wisdom in protecting yourself—to a point. But the defenses that keep out hurt can also hinder real intimacy with others. They can cause you to keep your emotional distance and even hold

back a part of your heart God intended for
your children.

There is a time to mourn. There is a time
to heal. There is a time to rejoice in new be-
ginnings. The key is allowing God to impart the
wisdom for each new season in its proper time.
Don't think for a minute He isn't working for and
with you. Even now He is softening your heart
and making it new. He's all about healing and
restoration.

So don't let fear hold you back from a fabu-
lous future. The Bible says God formed you
in your mother's womb. It says He has
a plan to give you hope. He's giving
it to you now, because you are
God's great gift to others.

You gain strength, courage, and confidence by every *experience* in which you really stop to look *fear* in the face . . . You must do the thing you cannot do.

—*Eleanor Roosevelt*

The eyes of every
woman in the gym
were on Becca.
Please let this be
a nightmare, and let
me wake up now!

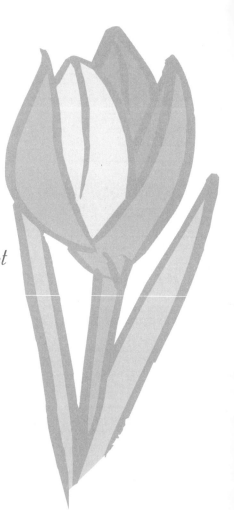

The Gift

Becca pulled her long brunette locks into a ponytail as she and her best friend, Constance, walked up the steps to the fitness center. "This was the worst idea of your entire life," Becca said through gritted teeth.

"A membership to the gym was the perfect birthday gift, whether you're willing to admit it or not," Constance countered. "It's not my fault you're the new member whose name was drawn to win free personal training with Dakota Davis, complete with before-and-after pictures in his new book."

They rounded a corner and stopped in front of a mob scene. More than thirty women flocked around an Adonis-like man autographing books.

"What's going on?" Becca asked.

"Dakota Davis, in the flesh," Constance said with a trace of awe. "He's signing his latest book."

"Not him," Becca said, staring. "Them." The women in the group wore tiny jogging bras and coordinating shorts, and shoes that evidently had never seen the light of day outside a gym. "They've all got makeup on!" Becca marveled. "Their hair is done. They're wearing jewelry!" Becca looked down at the baggy sweats and T-shirt she'd worn in an attempt to hide the effects of all the chocolate-chip cookie dough she'd eaten to relieve her stress.

"They dress that way because fitness centers are hot spots for meeting men," Constance explained.

Becca whirled around and looked at Constance through squinted eyes. "Is that what this is about?" she growled. "Are you trying to fix my love life again?"

"You don't have a love life," Constance said pointedly. "You've given me absolutely nothing to work with."

"Nor do I need one," Becca said in a huff.

"Look on the bright side," Constance said. "He's gorgeous, and he's single."

"He probably eats tofu and drinks raw-egg smoothies for breakfast!" Becca said with disgust.

The gym owner caught sight of Becca. "Here's our lucky winner," he announced.

The Gift

The eyes of every woman in the gym were on Becca as she stepped forward to shake hands with the fitness guru. Cameras flashed as a publicist snapped pictures. Becca whipped around to look for Constance, who had wisely left the building.

"The first thing on our agenda," Dakota explained, "is to determine your percentage of body fat."

Becca coughed, almost swallowing her chewing gum.

"I know the Heimlich maneuver," Dakota offered.

"No thanks, I'm all right," Becca said, gasping for air.

"We'll start first with measurements," he said, pulling out a measuring tape and wrapping it around Becca's hips. Becca could feel her face burn as she shifted uncomfortably.

"Now your waist," he said, stretching his arm around her.

Please let this be a nightmare, and let me wake up now!

"If you'll just step onto the scales," he said a few minutes later.

Becca looked around for a way out of the situation. *I could faint*, she thought.

"OK, up you go . . ."

Oh Lord, I'll never eat chocolate again if you'll just make these scales—

"Got it," Dakota said, writing numbers in his notebook. "I normally do underwater weighing to determine the percentage of body fat," he explained. "But since this gym doesn't have a tank, we'll do it the old fashioned way."

He grabbed a hunk of fat near her waist and pinched it with calipers while Becca plotted vengeance on Constance. She was exhausted long before the step test and weightlifting were over.

Dakota looked at the figures in his notebook. "This is going to take a lot of cardio," he said thoughtfully. "Cardio-vascular workouts are fat burners," he explained. "We'll start running day after tomorrow. How does that sound?"

"Oh . . . I'm sorry. I'm busy that day."

Dakota's right eyebrow rose. "For twenty-four hours?"

"Yes, I have a very demanding job."

"Really? What do you do?"

"I'm a children's book editor. So you see, I couldn't possibly . . ."

Dakota looked down at his paperwork. "I've got your address," he said. "I'm sure you get to go home sometime that night, so I'll stop by and we'll run in your neighborhood after dark." With a brilliant smile, he turned to wave good-bye to his many admirers.

Dakota Davis was the last thing on Becca's mind two evenings later when the doorbell rang. "Oh, it's you," Becca said as she opened the door. "Sorry, I can't run tonight."

The Gift

Dakota stepped inside before she could shut the door. "Look, I've got a book deal, and like it or not, you're part of the deal. So why don't we—"

"No, you look. I don't give a rip about your book. I've got a sick child, and that takes precedence over everything else, including you."

Surprise registered on Dakota's face. "You have a child?" he asked.

"Mommy!" At the plaintive wail, Becca turned and ran, Dakota on her heels.

Four-year-old Rachel lay propped up in bed with a cool cloth on her forehead. "Mommy, I feel worser!" she sobbed. Becca gathered the child in her arms.

"She's burning up," Dakota said, brushing a hand over Rachel's cheek. "Have you called the doctor?"

"Yes," Becca said, pulling out a thermometer. "There's a virus going around. He said it causes really high fevers, and I should try to keep it down. I was just about to take her temp again."

Moments later Becca read the digital thermometer. "It's almost 106!" she gasped. "We've got to get her to the emergency room!"

"There's no time. If it gets any higher, she could have seizures," Dakota said, taking Rachel from her arms. "Go to the nearest bathtub and start running cold water. I'm right behind you."

Rachel sobbed as Dakota lowered her into the icy water, but within a short time her fever began dropping. "Is it too soon to give her more Tylenol?" Dakota asked.

"No, it's time," Becca said, looking at her watch. "How do you know so much about kids? Do you have some of your own?"

"None of my own, but I'm the oldest of seven," he admitted with a shrug. "You learn a few things along the way."

Three hours later Rachel was asleep in her bed. Dakota followed Becca into the living room and dropped onto the sofa. "I feel like I just ran the Boston Marathon," he said. "Do you get up and go to work after nights like this?"

"Usually," Becca said. "As a single mom I have to work. But I'm fortunate that my mother lives nearby. She'll stay with Rachel while I work."

"You must have an amazing amount of stamina. Although it didn't show on your stress test," he said with a puzzled frown.

Becca pulled leftovers out of the refrigerator and began warming them. "A mother's stamina doesn't necessarily come from strong muscles," she said. "It's more a product of strong love." She pointed Dakota to a chair at the kitchen table, and he sat obediently.

"I think single parenting should be an Olympic event," he said with admiration.

Becca laughed as she put thick, homemade soup and bread on the table. Dakota watched in wide-eyed amazement as she slathered her bread with butter.

"Can you spell saturated fat?" he asked.

Becca smiled and smeared butter on his bread. "Live a little."

"That was delicious," Dakota said when they'd finished eating. "I'd rather eat a mother's cooking than that of the best chef in the world. I've never been able to understand why it tastes so good. My mom says it's because mothers mix love into all their recipes."

Becca laughed and started clearing the table. *That's not something I expected a Greek god to say.*

"Sit," Dakota ordered. "You look beat." Becca gratefully sat down while he filled the dishwasher.

"Let's talk about running," Dakota said, dropping into a chair beside her. "You can always run on a treadmill at the gym, but it's more interesting to run on the trails at the lake."

Becca blew her hair out of her eyes. "If I have to run, I would rather actually go somewhere," she said. "My problem is that I don't see how I can take any more time away from Rachel."

"We'll take her with us."

"Rachel? No, you probably didn't notice, but she has really short legs."

"Trust me. I'll meet you at the trails Saturday morning."

At the designated time, Dakota showed up with a jogger for Rachel. "Hello, Rachel," he said with a bow. "Your chariot awaits." Rachel giggled as he swung her into the jogger and fastened the straps.

Dakota showed Becca the correct way to jog and set a slow, easy pace while he pushed Rachel. "Rachel, look at the squirrel," he said, pointing at a nearby tree.

"Oh . . . he's so cute," Rachel cooed.

They jogged past sailboats coasting gracefully in the breeze. On a golf course to their left, golfers putted on thick green grass. Becca and Dakota talked about his new book and the children's book she planned to write. Before she knew it, they were back at her car.

"That was fun," she admitted.

"Becca, I'd like very much to take you to dinner tonight."

The Gift

"Another photo shoot?" she asked, lifting Rachel from the jogger.

"No, this has nothing to do with my book."

Becca used her sleeve to rub the sweat from her eyes. "Why then?" she asked.

Dakota seemed caught off guard. "Well, because I like you, and I want to spend time with you."

"With me?"

"Why does that surprise you?" he asked with a bemused smile.

"Because you've got all those women at the gym fawning over you," she said honestly.

"Posers," he said.

"I know they're not real athletes," Becca agreed. "But in case you haven't noticed, neither am I."

"That's not what I mean," Dakota said. "They're not posing as athletes. Most of them are posing as individuals. Instead of being their own persons, they pretend to be whatever they imagine men want them to be."

"Wow, that was pretty insightful," Becca said.

"It is possible to have both muscles and a mind." Dakota smiled. "Besides, weren't you impressed with my fawning females?"

"I remember thinking how strong you must be to withstand the wind from all those batting eyelashes," Becca retorted.

Dakota threw back his head and laughed. "I trust you to always keep me humble, in spite of my publicist's best efforts," he said, climbing into his car. "I'll pick you up at seven."

OK, maybe as gifts go, this one wasn't so bad.

Chapter 6

Giving
Guidance

When you dwell in the safety of My shelter, you'll find rest in the shadow of the Almighty. I'm loving toward you and faithful to everything I promise you. You can count on Me to complete the good work I've started in you and your family.

My forever love,
Your Trustworthy Father

—FROM PSALMS 91:1; 145:13; PHILIPPIANS 1:6

Sometimes, in the stress and strain of raising children, we lose sight of the final destination. Ready or not, it will come, that day when life's lessons have been learned—or not. But you are the one who gave your children their start on this journey called life. You are the one who helps them find their path, cheering them along the way.

All of the unexpected stops that slow them down on their road to success can cause you to take your weary eyes off the prize. Sometimes an especially trying stop may feel like the end of the line. Those are the times we need to regroup—to remember that maturity isn't birthed full grown, no matter how desperately we desire it to be. Sometimes it goes into remission for so long we fear it didn't survive.

Maturity in our children is often as illusive as the promise of spring during a long, hard winter. We're unable to see what's on the other side of the mountain as the train we ride chugs its way uphill. But remember, your words and your love are the guideposts that point the way to your children's final destination. You're the conductor who helps keep them on track and the whistle that warns of danger on the road ahead. You are the engine that drives them to greatness.

You are Mom. And you are the one who will rejoice when the journey's done.

A mother's love endures
through all; in good repute,
in bad repute, in the *face*
of the world's condemnation,
a *mother* still loves on.

—Washington Irving

Julia let out a long, slow sigh. At fifteen Nate had morphed into someone she didn't know.

Final Destination

It was still dark outside when Julia knocked on her son's bedroom door and peeked inside. "What?" Nate asked, his voice muffled by the pillow.

"Wake up, we're going to Texas."

"What about the transmission?" he asked groggily.

"We're going by train." The last thing Julia heard before closing Nate's door was, "Bogus." *I wonder if that's good or bad*, she thought as she went to wake six-year-old Chloe with kisses.

Two hours later Julia, Nate, and Chloe looked up at the massive locomotive shrouded in early morning fog. Even Chloe was speechless.

"All aboard!"

Giving *Guidance*

Julia lifted Chloe up the big step onto the train, and they wound their way up narrow stairs to the second-floor coach. The conductor turned two seats around so they could have four large seats facing one another. Julia stuffed their carry-on bags overhead while Nate reclined his seat, adjusted his headphones, turned up the volume, and closed his eyes. Chloe chattered for a while before crawling into Julia's lap and falling asleep. Julia leaned her head against the window and watched the countryside awaken.

Nothing in the world sounds as lonely as the horn of a train, she thought. At the mournful bellow she pulled Chloe closer and looked at Nate. He was awake, she felt sure. Instead of using his bedroom door as a barrier, as he did at home, he feigned sleep; his eyes fluttered behind closed lids, face set in rigid lines.

Julia let out a long, slow sigh. At fifteen Nate had morphed into someone she didn't know. He rarely left his room, spoke in monosyllables, and seemed to have headphones growing out of his ears; and Julia feared that sullen scowl he wore might be permanent. While Chloe was adjusting well to first grade, Julia felt as though she were losing Nate inch by miserable inch.

This whole vacation had been her desperate attempt to

reconnect with him. At her brother's ranch in Texas, Nate could camp and fish with his cousins while getting a big dose of family. *I just hope it's not too little too late.*

The train is a comfortable, leisurely way to travel, Julia thought as they pulled into a small town and took on more passengers. When she'd booked their tickets to Fort Worth, she'd had no idea of the dozens of small stops they'd make along the way. She might have made better time in a car, but with all of Chloe's bathroom and snack stops, she doubted it. And what a relief not to be at the wheel for hours on end.

All things considered, it was probably an easier trip for Nate and Chloe too. Instead of being confined by seat belts for hours on end, they could walk through the train, get snacks from the café, and visit with other kids. By late morning Chloe had already made friends with a little girl her age, and they'd each pulled a Barbie out of their backpacks to play.

The view out the window made Julia feel as though they were in some exotic country rather than rural American heartland. Thick green trees cast a cool shade onto the train as it wormed its way through a valley, with bright spots of sunlight shimmering through openings in the dense foliage.

"Nate, look at the view in this valley. You haven't used the digital camera yet—why don't you take some pictures of the trip?"

"Whatever . . ." Nate glared at Julia and then rolled his eyes before closing them again.

This is going well, Julia thought sarcastically. She set the camera on the empty seat beside Nate and picked up a book she'd brought. Absorbed in the story, she didn't notice Nate had picked up the camera until she heard the distinctive click as he snapped photos of the countryside.

Don't say anything, she warned herself, knowing from experience that trying to communicate with Nate would only drive him back into his shell. She hoped he didn't notice she wasn't turning pages. Glancing out the corner of her eye, she realized that he'd taken off his headphones and was making adjustments to the camera settings.

"Chloe, look up!" Nate said before snapping a picture of two grinning girls.

"Wait!" Chloe urged. "Get a picture of our Barbies!"

Nate hesitated only for a second before stretching to his full height and moving across the aisle to get a closeup of the Barbies dressed in evening attire.

"You want to see how they look?" he asked, kneeling beside the girls and letting them see the picture on the display screen.

"Cool," Chloe said.

"Nate, we're hungry. Would you take us down to the café so we can get something to eat?"

Julia didn't realize she'd been holding her breath until after Nate said, "OK." Then she let it out slowly. She felt rather than saw him turn toward her. *He needs money,* she thought, about to grab her purse. *Don't do that!* she scolded herself. *Wait until he asks. He needs to get back into the habit of talking to us.*

For several agonizing seconds there was silence between them as Julia forced her unfocused gaze on the pages of the book. Nate cleared his throat.

"Mom?"

Julia looked up at Nate as though surprised and gave him a blinding smile. "Yes, Son?"

"I've got money. You want anything from the snack bar?"

Julia wanted to lie down in the floor and cry. *He asked if I wanted something! How sweet is that?* "I'd love a bottle of water, Nate. Thanks."

"No problem," he said, turning to the girls. "Come on, squirt, let's go."

Giving *Guidance*

After they returned from the snack bar, the girls colored pictures and Nate put on his headphones. But this time his face didn't have that closed-off expression. Instead of closing his eyes, he alternately gazed out the window and flipped through a magazine.

Early in the evening, when they pulled into another small train station, the conductor announced that passengers could get off the train for a while if they wished. Nate, headphone in place and a computer game in hand, disappeared. It wasn't until the train had started moving that he returned to his seat.

"Mom, you won't believe what happened. I met the engineer, and he let me see the cab!"

Julia listened to her son describe the cab and the role of a train engineer. His headphones were around his neck, and his face was lit with excitement. It reminded her of the year he'd gotten an electric train for Christmas. He'd been about five years old.

"Did you know each state has its own speed limit for trains, just like they do for cars?" he asked. "For instance, in Oklahoma the speed limit is seventy-nine miles per hour, but when the train crosses the Red River into Texas, it drops to fifty-five. Right now we're going . . ."

He's making sentences! Julia thought. *He's talking in para-*

graphs! This may be the longest monologue of his life! Julia listened, enthralled, as the train rolled along the track. She reached for a bag and pulled out the blueberry muffins she'd made the day before.

"Ohhh . . . I love these babies," Nate crowed and bit enthusiastically into a large muffin. He finished it off in no time, then paused, looking thoughtful. "I've been thinking about going out for basketball next year in high school. I like soccer, but I think if I worked hard enough, I might have a chance at a basketball scholarship. And . . . well, don't laugh but . . ."

The sun dipped behind the horizon, and a hush fell over the train. Julia wrapped a blanket around Chloe, who'd fallen asleep in Nate's lap. He'd talked himself out and finally fell asleep while scratching Chloe's back.

Julia put her pillow against the window and looked out into the night. *Being Nate's mother has always been an adventure*, she thought with a smile. *And just like this train trip, there's no telling what stops he'll make on his journey to manhood.* But Julia felt confident that with lots of love and understanding, he would reach his final destination.

The train slowed, and the horn echoed across the valley. Strange, it was a comforting sound now.

Nate roused and stretched long, lean legs to rest socked feet in Julia's seat. "Mom," he said sleepily, "this isn't so bad."

"Bogus," she whispered.

Nate's lips twitched as he fought a smile, then he pulled his baseball cap over his eyes and slept.

Chapter 7

Finding
Love

I love you with an everlasting love and draw you to Me. Love is the greatest gift and the most excellent way to parent. As you mother, be patient and kind. Keep in mind that love isn't self-seeking or easily angered. Love makes sacrifices and rejoices in truth. Train your children with a love that always protects, always trusts, always believes, and never gives up.

My forever love,
Your Heavenly Father

—FROM JEREMIAH 31:3; 1 CORINTHIANS 12:31; 13:4–7

The heart is an amazing thing. It has the capacity to give all of itself away and then grow again from its own transplanted love. It has the ability to stretch itself past all natural boundaries and reach further still to express the essence of what's inside. A loving heart drives people to great exploits and grand victories. The heart is color-blind. It doesn't care about social status or bank accounts, because deep calls to deep, and the call of a heart is to love.

The heart is the reason families come in so many different sizes and shapes. Love simply will not be put in a box. It makes a family of a wise old man with a wrinkled face and a troubled teen who needs a strong hand to guide him. It takes broken lives and puts them back together seamlessly as a family. Just as ocean waves sweep onto shore and then flow back out to sea, removing all tracks and trash from the sand and leaving pristine beaches, so love sweeps back and forth over our hearts, healing, mending, and restoring.

Love sets the solitary in families. Love makes a way when there seems to be no way. Of all the things you've done for your child, only one is a living essence that will grow and multiply for generations to come: love. It was not your hand that made your house a home, knitting your family's hearts securely into one; it was your love.

The richest source of *healing*
our loneliness is for us to
begin to *give* ourselves in love.

–Robert A. Williams

Heather looked at Michael, whose eyes had closed in sleep. "Both of our lives are at a crossroads."

The Verdict

Heather walked into her law office and stopped abruptly. The plush waiting room looked like a tornado had swept through it. The phone was ringing and the secretary was bouncing a crying baby on her lap.

Heather's law partner, Donna, stepped out of her office, silk blouse wrinkled and hair mussed. "Thank God, you're back! We need to talk!" Then, as an afterthought, she whirled around. "Oh, my goodness—you're back! What was the verdict?"

A slow grin spread across Heather's face. "We won! They awarded ten million in damages."

Donna dropped into the nearest chair. Her secretary slammed down the phone. For a moment even the baby stopped crying.

"Ten million . . . ," Donna repeated. Lunging from her chair, she threw herself into Heather's arms. "You did it! We need to celebrate! I can't believe I'm leaving for Cancun tonight."

"We'll celebrate when you get back," Heather said with an easy smile. "What's with the baby?" As if on cue, the baby—a red-cheeked cherub about nine months old—started crying.

"Let me see if I've got this straight," Heather summarized several minutes later. "Some woman found us listed in the yellow pages under Family Law."

Donna nodded. "That's right."

"Then she showed up here with her baby and asked to have her parental rights severed because she could no longer provide for the child?"

"Right. She was afraid if she went through social services, her son would be put into foster care and never be adopted into a permanent family."

"You went before a judge this afternoon, and he terminated the mother's parental rights?"

"Yes. The young father had already terminated his."

"So now you have to find a suitable family to adopt the baby?"

"That's right."

"But you're leaving the country for two weeks. Who's going to keep him while you're gone?"

"That's one loose end I still have to tie up. He doesn't have a passport, so I can't take him out of the country with my family. So far everyone I've called is on vacation. I've put a call in to a nanny service, and they're trying to find someone who'll take Michael in until we find him a family."

"I have an idea," Heather offered impetuously. "I'll take him until you get back."

"You?"

"How hard could one baby be?"

"I don't know, Heather."

"Did you forget that I just won a ten-million-dollar verdict? Surely a baby can't be worse than six grueling months of litigation. I'd already decided to take some time off, so I'll be home anyway. As soon as you get back, we'll find a more permanent solution."

"Wow," Donna said, sighing with relief. "That would solve a huge problem for me. I was beginning to think I'd have to send Charles on to Cancun with the kids until I could find someone to take care of Michael. Thanks, Heather. I've already ordered everything he'll need for a couple of weeks, so I'll have it delivered to your house. Charge anything else he needs to the firm."

Finding *Love*

That evening Heather looked with wide-eyed disbelief at the mountain of paraphernalia in her living room. "One baby couldn't possibly need all those things!"

Michael let loose a bloodcurdling wail.

"Oh . . . I'm guessing you're hungry."

Arms trembling from being unaccustomed to the weight of a baby, Heather read the instructions for the third time before testing the formula to make sure it wasn't too hot. Her high-tech kitchen was littered with formula, bottles, juice, and baby food of what seemed like every possible variety.

Baby and bottle in hand, Heather looked around her contemporary living room. *I'm getting a rocking chair*, she decided. Piling pillows high onto her bed, she snuggled into them and smoothed the baby's damp hair back from his face as he drank hungrily from the bottle. Large brown eyes stared up at her. Her heart leaped as a tiny hand clamped on to her finger.

"I wonder how you bathe a baby?" she asked, but Michael just stared at her, unblinking. A while later, when she set him in a sink full of warm bathwater, he immediately slapped his hands into the bath, spraying Heather's face and hair with sudsy water.

"I think you've pulled that trick before," Heather said, afraid to take her hands off of him to wipe her face. She soaped his soft skin, then rinsed him and placed him on a large, soft towel.

He crawled away before she could grab him.

"Come back here!" She caught him from behind. *This has to be a lot like pig wrestling*, Heather thought as she fought to get a diaper and nightshirt on Michael.

When she finally tucked him into the portable crib that evening, she turned on the baby monitor so she could hear him in her room. Heather crawled into bed and quickly fell asleep to the sound of Michael's soft snore.

The next thing she knew, Heather was bolting upright out of a deep sleep. Her digital clock flashed 2:38 a.m. What was that awful noise? She dashed to the guest room and found Michael standing in his crib, sobbing. His chubby fists reached for her as she lifted him from the crib.

"Come here, sweetie," she said, pulling him to her chest and feeling his tears soak through her pajama top. His face was flushed and he felt warm to the touch. She dug through the baby supplies and found a thermometer. He had a low-grade fever.

Oh, Lord. I was sure I could handle a baby. But a sick baby is another story.

She paced the floor, trying to remember all the fevers her nieces and nephews had survived. What should she do?

Call a doctor? Take him to the emergency room?

She seized upon a distant memory: Her sister was holding a crying, feverish baby. She rubbed a finger over his gums and announced, "He's teething."

Teething. Could this be nothing more than a painful tooth? She sat on the sofa and rubbed a finger over Michael's gums until she felt the point of a tooth trying to shove its way into the world. Michael bit on her finger and stopped crying. His big eyes still brimming with tears, he bit harder on her finger and leaned his head against her shoulder.

With her free hand she pawed through the things Donna had had delivered until she found something to rub on his gums and something to help both the discomfort and the fever. Half an hour later they both fell into an exhausted sleep.

The next morning Michael ate breakfast hungrily, never taking his eyes off Heather. Holding him on one hip, she cleaned the kitchen and made a pot of coffee. Michael clung to her when the furniture store delivered the rocking chair. She folded his clothes and put them in a dresser, set up the rocker and the swing in the living room, and piled his toys in a small chest.

"Just like a man," Heather said, feeding him carrots. "You're here for less than twenty-four hours, and you've already taken over the place. I suppose next you'll want the remote control." His crooked grin confirmed her thought.

She wiped Michael's face and sat in the rocker. "When my life is turned upside down, I usually have a chocolate binge or a good cry, but maybe you'd just like to rock." He sighed and relaxed against her arm as soft music played in the background. The rhythmic creak of the rocking chair was almost hypnotic. Heather breathed in the baby's scent and thought about her fiancé, who'd died in a helicopter crash five years earlier.

What would my life be like now if he'd lived? Would we have a passel of kids?

She probably wouldn't have just won a ten-million-dollar verdict. But while that victory took her career as a trial attorney to a whole new level, her heart and home felt empty at the end of a long day. She looked down at Michael, whose eyes had fluttered closed in sleep.

"Both of our lives are at a crossroads," she said, closing her own eyes and leaning her head against the back of the rocker.

Heather was amazed at how quickly the days with Michael were passing. Donna would be back soon. That thought made Heather feel anxious.

She put Michael on the floor and placed several toys just out of his reach. He crawled straight to the red ball and whacked it with all his strength. "So you're already into sports?" Heather asked, rolling the ball toward him. Michael threw his head back and chortled with delight, and Heather felt her heart flop in her chest.

"Don't toy with me," she said. "The sound of your laughter could become addictive."

As Heather reached for the ball, Michael grabbed the sofa and pulled himself up. "Here it is!" Heather exclaimed. Michael let go of the sofa. With wide eyes and his mouth forming a perfect *O*, he took a step. Heather held her breath as he took a second. The third step brought him close enough to grab the ball.

But he walked past it and lunged into Heather's arms. Wrapping his little arms around her, he held on tightly and laughed so hard he shook all over. His laughter echoed into every empty corner of her heart.

That night Donna called from Mexico to check in. "How's it going?"

"We've stumbled onto the perfect therapy for a homeless baby and a war-torn attorney," Heather said. "We rock. Sleep, food, and diaper changes are nothing more than brief interruptions. The pace is perfect for both of us."

The Verdict

"I can't thank you enough for all you've done," Donna said. "I'll find him a home soon."

"You already have," Heather said. "Michael is home."

"Heather!"

"Donna, since Collin died the jury's been out on my having a family," Heather explained. "But now we have a verdict. I was here for Michael's first step. I want to watch him throw his first ball. I want to hold his hand and walk him into first grade. I want this child to feel loved every day of his life."

"What if Mr. Right comes along?" Donna asked.

"Mr. Right would recognize a good package deal when he saw one," Heather said. She watched Michael pick up the television remote. Sticking it in his mouth, he gnawed it with a new tooth. By some testosterone-driven instinct, he clicked on the sports channel, and then sighed with total contentment. Heather understood the feeling.

"It's great to win at trial," she continued, looking at Michael with growing love. "But it's even better to win at life. And I just hit the jackpot."

Journal about the blessings or challenges of being a single mom . . .

_____

_____

_____

_____

_____

_____

_____

_____

_____

_____

_____

_____

_____

_____

_____

_____

_____

_____

_____

_____

_____